A Pea Coat Goes Home

Les Rolston

A Pea Coat Goes Home
Copyright © 2015 by **Les Rolston**.
All rights reserved.

No part of this publication may be reproduced, stored in a retrieval system or transmitted in any way by any means, electronic, mechanical, photocopy, recording or otherwise, without the prior permission of the author except as provided by USA copyright law.

The opinions expressed by the author are not necessarily those of Revival Waves of Glory Books & Publishing.

Published by Revival Waves of Glory Books & Publishing
PO Box 596| Litchfield, Illinois 62056 USA
www.revivalwavesofgloryministries.com

Revival Waves of Glory Books & Publishing is committed to excellence in the publishing industry.

Book design copyright © 2015 by Revival Waves of Glory Books & Publishing. All rights reserved.

EBook: 978-1-943845-40-8

Paperback: 978-0692490877

PUBLISHED IN THE UNITED STATES OF AMERICA

Dedication

This book is dedicated to the men and women of the United States Navy.

Acknowledgement

This book would not have been possible without the love and support of my wife, Elaine Ann Savini.

A Pea Coat Goes Home

When I was six years-old I discovered a big wooden box in our family's attic. My fourteen year-old sister opened it for me—it was a treasure trove. The 2 ½' by 5' chest was full of faded photos, yellowing letters and full-length fur coats. Confounded but curious I picked through the smaller mementos and trinkets from the 1930s and 40s and breathed the stale hot air of the attic perfumed with the aroma of cedar. I found a pair of sailors' pants with *so* many buttons on the front that I thought of the iconic cartoon character Popeye. In a few years I would wear them to high school.

At the bottom of the chest was a dark-blue heavy coat. Even at that tender age, I was moved by it. Its silk lining was pristine; it bore no stains or tears. It felt good in my hands. I wanted it. That night at dinner, I worked up the courage to ask my dad if I could have it and with a degree of sweetness mixed with disinterest he said, "Sure, when you're old enough." He didn't tell me what it was.

"Old enough" became ninth grade and the coat kept me warm as I turned up its collar on my mile long trek to high school on windy February mornings. My friends envied and wanted my coat. It was so unusually stylish that no one would dare steal it because its ownership was never in doubt. It was "military" but still somehow "cool" in spite of the unpopular war in Viet Nam. It was forever mine. I wore it through winter winds and rain and the occasional muddy touch-football game after school. Rain-soaked music festivals in the years that followed didn't dissuade my love of the old coat—it was my personal suit of armor. By my late-twenties I had grown a bit taller than my father had been in his navy days and the old coat was once again retired. It would hang in various closets for the next forty years.

This is the story of my father, me, and an old coat.

My father loved the ocean. Looking back it seems funny because he taught me how to snare fish with a line of string and dive in his childhood swimming hole near a land-locked place called Tyler Hill in eastern Pennsylvania. He grew up as a farm boy and had never seen an ocean. His name was Ken. He was athletic, strong, seemingly fearless, and loved to make people laugh. "Kenny" left school in eighth grade to help his father, Earl, work the family dairy farm. Throughout his life he was always embarrassed about his lack of formal education.

I went into the building business with him in Rhode Island decades later and when we would meet with architects, engineers and developers he was often the smartest person in the room – but he didn't know it. The challenges of farm life forced him to be hardworking, innovative and creative. During the energy crisis of the mid-1970s, Ken thought it would be wise to put individual thermostats in four different rooms of our modest home. Plumber after plumber looked at the job at hand and he was told it couldn't be done because there was only one boiler. He devised and built his own system and within two weeks it was working. Not being able to comprehend what my father was talking about I contributed little to the effort. How was I supposed to know how to solder a copper pipe? My father would get impatient with me, but never lost his temper—after all, his kid didn't have the *opportunity* to grow up on a working farm during the Great Depression. I never told him how proud I felt of him that day. How could he be *so* smart anyway? The current owners of the old house tell me that the four- zone heating system still works perfectly and plumbers scratch their heads and marvel when they're called to unclog a drain.

Being of humble beginnings my father was not prone to exaggeration. He became easily irritated by those who had tendencies to embellish their own personal stories. He referred to them as artists of a "particular" genre. Well, that isn't exactly what he called them, but it meant the same thing.

I worked with my Dad for the better part of three decades. Sometimes we had crews, but usually it was just the two of us. We framed houses, remodeled kitchens and installed roofs. There wasn't much we didn't do actually. I don't know how many hours we spent together in his pickup truck but it must have been in the thousands. Some days we'd talk and some days we'd be too busy or tired.

We'd talk mostly baseball, family and work. Occasionally an item we heard on the news provided me the opportunity to ask him about the war because he would never be the first to talk about it. We once spent six weeks working on the home of a former shipmate of his and neither of them mentioned the subject even once. But when I asked my father questions he shared detailed and thoughtful remembrances devoid of emotion. It was as if he really wanted me to know the story and not let it be blurred by his personal sadness and loss. I always felt he was telling me about some movie he had watched on television the night before. I hung on his every word. In later years I did my own research on his experiences and they were dead-on with what he had told me.

As a teenager I got to know how his family lived back in the 1920s. The kids: Ruth, my father Kenny, Les, and little brother Roy would be roused early, about 4:30, by their mother Louise. In the winter the heated bricks each child went to bed with the night before were cold by dawn. No one wanted to get up but there were chores to get done. There were cows to milk and hogs to be slopped before trekking off to school. On this mission Ruth, Kenny and Les would lead the way with Roy struggling to keep up.

A few years ago I visited my cousin Sharyn and her husband Bill in Waymart, Pennsylvania. As we talked I told her how I always wondered about the long walk our parents made to school every day. So Sharyn and I decided to drive to the old farm and once and for all determine how long that daily commute had been for these kids who had been our parents, aunts and uncles. We reminded each other how things from our own childhood always seemed bigger and farther away than they actually were. I recalled being a little boy and being enchanted by these hilly dirt roads and woods a half-century earlier.

Sharyn and I said little else as we drove along in her van. It was my favorite moment with her. The odometer rolled over to a mile, then two. Could I have done this as a little kid? Could I do it *now*? We arrived at the former site of the little schoolhouse after driving over *three and a half* miles. I couldn't imagine that hike in the dead of winter. My Aunt Ruth told me many years ago, "It wasn't so bad. In the winter, once and a while a neighboring farmer would hitch up his sleigh and we'd laugh all our way to school. But sometimes on the way to school, we'd be interrupted by a black bear or a loose bull." After school there were more chores and homework to tend to. My father never lost the work ethic he developed as a child and I marveled at how he could work so tirelessly.

In his late-teens Ken became infatuated with motorcycles. He was always riding and even if you couldn't *see* him you could *hear* him. His motorcycle was his pride and joy and his brothers and friends couldn't resist having fun with his new obsession. One morning Ken woke to discover that his prized bike was missing. "No one knew nothing" and he spent most of the day searching around Tyler Hill to no avail. Not suspecting that he had been the victim of a prank he began driving his father's car back to the farm as the sun was setting. In the distance he spied an unusual shape in a tree. At the time he didn't find the situation funny and a photograph survives as evidence of the "motorcycle in a tree" episode. All was forgiven, but his own passion for such good-natured pranks was stoked.

A young Kenny Rolston retrieving his motorcycle (circa. 1938)

Unlike a lot of my friends in the summer of 1969 I didn't go to the famed Woodstock music festival in Bethel, New York, which was only an hour away from the old farm which by then was owned by my Uncle Roy. Instead, I helped my uncle bring in his hay; it became my summer ritual. Eventually I would bring a few friends for the same purpose. The neighboring farmers would gawk at these "long-hairs" piling hay bales on the trailer my Uncle Roy was pulling along on his tractor ahead of us.

My friends and I always slept in the barn, raising Uncle Roy to suspicion. "Don't you city slickers smoke in my haymow! I'm tellin' you boys, don't you burn down my barn!" That is my tangible connection to my father's childhood. Yes, the barn is still there.

The farm as it looks today

On December 7, 1941, my father was 21 years old. Although the Japanese attack on the U.S. navy base at Pearl Harbor inspired both Ken and his brother Les to join the service they would have to wait until younger brother Roy was capable enough to work the farm with their father. On March 26, 1942, my father drove 50 miles along a winding road high above the Delaware River to the city of Port Jervis, New York, to enlist. His brother Les joined the army later that year. Ken was soon on his way to Rhode Island to train at the Quonset Point Naval Air Station. In addition to his work and dress uniforms he was issued a heavy wool, silk-lined pea coat to ward off the cold and bracing winds. He was wearing it when he met my aunt-to-be, "Reenie", on a blind date in Providence on a chilly April evening. They liked each other, but neither of them felt "the magic." She suggested that he ask her sister Shirley out. He did and there *was* magic. Their fledgling romance was cut short by Ken's transfer from Newport to Chicago on May 16 where he would continue his training. The two wrote letters and their fondness for each other was locked in envelopes which were routinely unlocked by the government. They didn't care. They wanted the world to know about their new-found love.

When Ken enlisted in the navy his ambition was to be where the action was—a machine gunner on a dive bomber. He once told me a story as to how this dream was never realized and that he and his classmates were given a surprise day off. He and most of the guys went to a bar to "let off a little steam." To their horror they were given another surprise the following morning—the dreaded machine gunner's test! Most of the men failed, including my father. But recently I found a note in his navy medical records that revealed my Dad's white lie to his boy. In spite of all his physical abilities, he had failed an eye exam. I'm sure he never told my mother and I never saw him wearing glasses. But I know he must have been devastated. He had to *settle* for a position as an airplane mechanic and was assigned to the VT-16 training squadron on January 8, 1943.

Ken had never been so far from the farm and never away for so long. But his life was about to take a positive turn. He was assigned to a newly christened ship which was to embark on shakedown cruises in the spring. He missed the lady he had left behind in Providence, Rhode Island, and thought that his new assignment would take them even farther apart. Then he heard his orders, "Men, you're going to Boston." Even in 1943 Boston to Providence was only a 90 minute train ride.

On April 5, 1943, he glimpsed another lady for the first time and she would be his home for the next two years, six months and eighteen days, *Lady Lex*. April in Boston can be cold and windy, especially in the morning, and a warm coat is a necessity. A pea coat is a luxury.

The aircraft carrier *Lexington* was launched from the Bethlehem Steel Corporation in Quincy, Massachusetts, on September 23, 1942, and was commissioned four months later with the amiable Captain Felix Stump in command. It was the fifth United States naval vessel to carry the name of the famous Revolutionary War battle. Earlier in the war the U.S.S. *Lexington* CV-2 had been sunk. This new *Lexington* was designated CV-16 and was the largest moving object my father had ever seen. Her deck is the equivalent of over three football fields in length, 150 feet wide and capable of carrying 110 aircraft. Fully loaded she displaces 36,380 tons and can be home to 2,600 officers and enlisted men; the biggest group my father had ever been a part of. Once underway this wide-eyed farm boy was awed by her speed, power and range. He was now an aviation machinist mate and working on planes called Hellcats, Avengers and Dauntless Dive Bombers filled his days. Milking cows and bringing in the hay would never again be part of his life.

The *Lexington* CV-16 is launched at Quincy, Massachusetts, September 23, 1942.

The crew shook the bugs off the *Lex* throughout the spring and summer of 1943 enjoying the sights and breezes of the

Caribbean until passing through the Panama Canal to join the rest of her fleet in the Pacific as part of Task Force-58. A task force consisted of as many as two dozen destroyers, cruisers and various support vessels. The ships sailed in a ring protecting the aircraft carrier at the center. The *Lexington* arrived at Pearl Harbor on August 9, 1943, and by late September her planes fired their first shots in anger; raiding Japanese air bases on the island of Tarawa. By fall the *Lex* was fully engaged in the Wake and Gilbert Islands' operations where her planes shot down 29 enemy aircraft in a 48 hour period.

My father told me how hard he and the other machinists worked to keep *their* planes in the air as they returned with varying degrees of damage. Any plane that could not be repaired and posing a danger to the other returning aircraft were simply hauled overboard. Commanding these machinists was hard-nosed Ensign V.A. Prather, whose growling voice spewed out endless obscenity laced tirades—nothing was ever fixed fast enough or good enough but the men held a grudging respect for their boss. My father told me that he once saw a man walk into a spinning propeller cutting him in half. Prather immediately started barking orders such as, "What the f*** are you looking at? Clean this sh** up!" It was Prather's job to keep the men alert, and alive.

Ken befriended another machinist mate who also came from a rural background named Jack who also had a Rhode Island sweetheart. Ken and Jack usually worked their craft on the hangar deck below, escaping the blazing South Pacific sun. The first time the *Lex* came under air attack, they couldn't resist getting a peek at what was until then a phantom enemy. Getting topside, they saw Japanese Zeros "swarming like bees." As one Zero approached the fantail of the ship he could see the pilot's face. The pilot opened up his machine guns and began strafing the deck near where Jack and my father were standing. "We realized right then that these guys meant business and we scrambled back down to the hangar deck."

Occasionally one of the *Lexington's* pilots would get shot down or "splashed." The lucky ones would bail out and be rescued by a destroyer. These rescues turned into a ritual. The destroyer would pull alongside the *Lexington* and a cable carrying a basket would be connected to the two vessels and the pilot would be returned to the carrier via this clothesline-like device. But this exchange was never free and the *Lexington* would return the basket filled with gallons of ice cream or other treats.

In early December the *Lexington* was near Kwajalein Island. She scored big again as her planes destroyed a freighter and damaged two cruisers; 30 Japanese fighters were shot out of the sky. The planes were the responsibility of my father and other machinists as well as the officers in the air department. The bond between pilot and machinist bordered on sacred as the pilots' safety and their planes' performance rested in the hands of the machinist mates—they were a team. To solidify this relationship the pilots would frequently ask their machinists, "Whaddaya say, take her upstairs?" As a young boy, my father told me how excited he was to feel the roar of the engine from *inside* the cockpit as the pilot taxied on the flight deck waiting for the signal to launch. He felt a rush of adrenaline as the plane roared toward the end of the flight deck which, "looked like the edge of the world" then "up, up, up into the clouds!" The pilots were not thanking their machinists for their work with these excursions, but instead were assuring themselves that these machinists were confident enough in their own work to get on board. After climbing to an altitude of over five miles the pilot would ask my father, "What should we do now, Kenny?" These were the words the former Pennsylvania farm boy would come to dread.

Reaching a top speed of two hundred and fifty miles per hour the pilot would put the Dauntless into a screeching dive—the surface of the ocean was coming up quicker and quicker. In terrified silence my father was thinking, "Pull up, please pull UP!" Every time, it seemed, just before what he thought was to be certain impact, he could hear and feel the plane groan as the pilot pulled her nose up. Suddenly they were soaring only a few feet above the water to launch an imaginary torpedo at an imaginary enemy ship. The hayfields suddenly looked pretty good in my father's mind.

Then it was up into the clouds again for the real test of the machinist's work. Flying upside down and a few "Loop De Loops" satisfied the pilot's endless quest for maneuverability. Then it was back to the *Lex*. As the plane approached the stern of the carrier and the flight deck, my woozy father was once again certain that he was about to die thinking, "Coming in too low, TOO LOW!" Before he could finish his vision of demise, the Dauntless's tail-hook snagged the arresting wires; the plane jerked back like a paddleball. Climbing out of the cockpit the pilot would express his concerns with the plane and add, "Nice job, Kenny." My father always acted completely unfazed.

A Dauntless Dive Bomber snags the arresting gear.

A safe return

There was plenty of downtime aboard this floating city. As in peacetime, men always seemed to make friends with others who shared similar interests such as chess, religious affiliations, and sports. Mail was the common thread, often arriving late or not at all. My father wrote countless letters to my mom which routinely arrived opened with pages missing or lines blackened out—"Loose lips sink ships" rang painfully true and the government scanned all mail for anything that might aid the Japanese should it come into their possession. My mother anguished endlessly over where her husband-to-be was and where he was going. The farm boy who never went to high school knew how to allay her worries—my father had a plan. It was devised before he left Quonset, Rhode Island, and they would hide nothing from the navy; their code would be right on the front of the envelope. His name was Kenneth E. Rolston, but if heading to Hawaii it would be Kenneth *"H"* Rolston. Pearl Harbor would be *"P"*, Washington *"W"* and on it went. My mother dreaded receiving a *"J"* letter.

Having grown up on a working farm my father was quite strong for his 5' 9" frame and extremely quick with his hands. His love of competition naturally drew him to the *Lexington's* boxing team where he had more than reasonable success. I remember him telling me how he once got to fight one of the contenders for the fleet welterweight championship. Awestruck, I asked him what happened. Smiling at me he said, "I got knocked out," obviously proud of himself for getting in the ring at all.

Down time

Ken was a friendly sort and easily approachable with a passion for having a good time. You had to work at making him not like you. On the farm the nearest neighbor was a mile away or more. *Lady Lex* opened his eyes to the world and he took it in with a quiet curiosity. He was now interacting with men of various ethnic backgrounds and cultures with varying degrees of education.

One day there was a sudden burst of excitement on the side of the flight deck. Like everyone else he ran over to see what all the commotion was about. Mechanics were throwing hammers and wrenches at something in the water. Pushing through the mob, he reached the port side and looked down. Floating in the water below was a terrified Japanese pilot who had been shot down earlier in the day.

The *Lexington* under attack. The smoke is from Japanese planes being shot down.

The deck officers quelled the crowd and made room for the enemy pilot to be hoisted aboard and escorted to the brig below. After extensive questioning the man was fed, allowed to bathe and put in a cell. The next day Ken met this man, who, in my father's mind, only purpose in life was to kill American sailors. The meeting was awkward as the pilot was in the act of relieving himself and using a single piece of toilet paper. At witnessing the legendary strict discipline of the Japanese navy my father pushed a full roll through the bars in a gesture of good will and left the man in private.

A few minutes later Ken returned to try to communicate with the man who he thought might as well have been from another planet. "How can I talk to this guy?" my father thought to himself. Hand signals maybe? The prisoner remained stone-silent. As my father turned to leave the pilot suddenly spoke his own name. Then he spoke again—in English! "He talked better English than *me*," my dad said. The pilot explained to my father how much he loved the United States, particularly Boston and the Red Sox, and how he had lived there for several years until his graduation from Harvard University. Their conversation was brief. I've been told that in wartime people briefly pass in and out of each others' lives, leaving memories that sometimes linger for years. This was one such encounter.

Another eye-opening moment came one afternoon as a dozen or so sailors lazed about on the flight deck. Men would come and go as my father napped. Upon awakening, he found that there was only one other man with him who was also stirring—an African-American. At that time, men of color were relegated to the duty of mess attendant, but conversations between shipmates seldom concerned their separate assignments. These young men were of a similar thread—striving to stay alive and longing for home. There was a seemingly endless ocean surrounding them. Hours and hours of boredom punctuated by sudden moments of terror and surrealism filled their days, weeks and months. I don't recall the man's name but my father spoke of him several times. Machinist Mate Rolston and his mess attendant friend shared stories and pictures of loved ones under the South Pacific sun—a trust was built. "Kenny, are you hungry?" became a running inside joke between the two. But this was no ordinary mess mate, this was the admiral's chef! There were always a couple of filet mignons or lobsters about to go to waste. To this day I wish I had paid closer attention to this story. As a little boy, my mother and father instilled in me their own abhorrence of bigotry, "You'll only miss out on meeting a lot of good people," I was warned. That was the greatest gift my parents ever gave me. If I could find my father's culinary partner-in-crime I would love to take him to dinner.

AMM2c Kenneth Rolston

(right) during exercise on the flight deck of the U.S.S. *Lexington* CV-16

Keeping cool

The ancient game of mumblety-peg was a popular pastime for the crew of the *Lexington*. It would be played on the flight deck where opponents would throw jackknives between their own feet. After several turns the man who stuck a knife closest to his own foot would win and the loser would have to pull the knife out of the wooden deck with his teeth. Obviously this didn't please the ship's dentist but the games continued in spite of their disapproval.

Ken and much of the crew routinely listened to a Japanese radio program called "Zero Hour" which featured an American-born woman who went by the name Orphan Ann. My dad told me that her propaganda based show was directed at American servicemen and she would talk about Allied setbacks and defeats. To the chagrin of the government her reports were often true. Over the ship's crackling intercom system Orphan Ann would continuously plant seeds of doubt into the minds of soldiers and sailors asking, "What do you think your girl back home is doing tonight? Do you really think she will wait for you?" But she played American popular music more contemporary than what was played on the Armed Forces Network so the Navy reluctantly allowed its men to listen to the Zero Hour. Her taunts and rants were ignored and the music made listening worthwhile. Orphan Ann was more commonly known as "Tokyo Rose."

Whatever impact she had on the morale of the crew aboard the *Lexington* there *were* men desperate to go home. My father once told me of a sailor who would walk around dragging a hot dog on a string talking to it saying, "Good boy" or "heel." Other men would go to more serious lengths hoping for a Section 8 (mentally unfit) discharge.

On December 4, 1943, morning came early for the men of the *Lexington's* air department. Pilots, machinists mates and all crew members involved with flight deck operations rolled out of their bunks at 3:40. The ship's messmen began their day over an hour earlier. On this morning, the Lexington's planes were to attack Japanese positions on Kwajalein Island. When I was in my late teens my father described the events of that day while we were driving to a construction site. Battle Breakfast consisted of steak, ham, eggs, home fries and gallons and gallons of coffee. At 6 AM he assured his pilot that his plane was good to go. Thirty minutes later the planes were in the air, although some would soon return within minutes due to mechanical problems. My father remembered how a cocky, fun-loving pilot named Rucinski smiled at him as he jumped out of an oil leaking Hellcat and ran across the flight deck to climb aboard another that was warmed up and ready to fly. With a confident smile my dad explained to me, "You can't be a pilot without an airplane."

The Kwajalein Raid was a huge success for the *Lexington's* Air Department. Thirty enemy planes were shot down and two cruisers were badly damaged. A supply ship, the *Kemba Maru* was also sunk. The *Lexington* suffered no losses and by dusk all of her planes had safely returned and their crews were being debriefed, eating and ready to crawl into their bunks. The machinist mates were inspecting, repairing and refueling their planes. Under a cloudless night the men assembled the planes on the flight deck not knowing what morning might bring.

A full moon reflected brightly off a calm South Pacific. In the distance one of the *Lexington's* sister ships, the U.S.S. *Yorktown*, could be seen. In spite of this serenity the mood of my father and the rest of the crew grew tense — they knew they had badly stung the Japanese navy and they were deep into *their* territory. As the crew settled in for the evening there was a sense of uneasiness. It was unusually quiet as men wrote letters and played cards below deck while others indulged in games of Mumblety-peg on the flight deck. Mostly everyone had a feeling that this day was not yet done.

At 7:30, radar indicated that dozens of Japanese planes were closing in on the *Lexington* from several directions. To guard against a torpedo attack on the ship's propellers and rudders a battleship pulled up behind. The quiet on the carrier faded into near silence except in the radar room and on the bridge. The acclaimed photographer, Edward Steichen, was on the bridge and remembered that Captain Stump paced anxiously in these moments. Around 8 o'clock friendly fire was heard from the western horizon. An hour later the task force began firing its five-inch guns into the sky. My father told me he saw no enemy planes and the photographer said, "[It looked as if we were] shooting at the moon."

About 9:15 a bright yellow glare appeared on the horizon and instantly disappeared. It was a Japanese plane shot out of the sky. The buzz throughout the ship was, "They are coming!" Thirty-five minutes later Japanese planes lit up the horizon by dropping flares. The blazing moonlight and the flares exposed the task force as if it were a sunny spring afternoon. The photographer remembered how he watched in awe, "I pay very little attention to the reports that planes are 20 miles away, but when 3 miles away … and closing in … something tries to crowd up in my chest."

My dad said he felt the *Lexington* suddenly slow down and change course. At about eleven o'clock the *Lexington* opened fire. The constant booming of anti-aircraft fire was felt everywhere on the ship. The photographer probably captured the moment better with words than any camera could, "All hell is let loose around us. This moon is no neutral bystander, starkly it points out our ships to the enemy. I can see [our ships] as plainly as daylight. How I hate that smooth, bland moon, [I] want to scratch it down, blast it to smithereens. A frightened young officer [near me said aloud], 'Damn that moon.'"

Men stood quietly at their battle stations as men below deck silently or openly prayed. Never a religious man I assume my father was thinking of my mother, but I never dared to ask. Twenty tense minutes passed when four flares slowly descended by parachute around the *Lexington*. Everyone aboard knew what this meant. Japanese torpedo planes were closing in and the *Lexington* was the target—alone. Captain Stump held his breath waiting for the flares to burn out and he ordered a defensive Zig-Zag course which the entire crew felt. "At least we are doing something," my father thought. For the first time in over four hours the tension on the carrier eased up just a little as it appeared that the brilliant moonlight and the glowing flares had confused the Japanese pilots as to the *Lexington's* position. My father told me it was as if the entire crew exhaled at once.

At 11:30 three or four enemy planes were seen bearing down on the carrier's starboard bow—the *Lexington's* guns awoke in a fury. "Les," my father said, staring at me with a seriousness I had seldom seen, "there was this deafening roar and a shudder— men were thrown out of their bunks or knocked off their feet like they were in a hurricane. At the same moment the rear of the ship rose high out of the water. Stuff was flying everywhere. As if in slow motion the ship settled and everything went silent except for the ship itself that seemed to groan like a sick lion. We couldn't see anything and the smell of smoke and oil filled our compartment. Really, the ship seemed to go up in the air." It was bad. The *Lexington's* rudders had been struck by a torpedo, steering control was lost and some men began to prepare to abandon ship.

One of the *Lexington's* rudders was completely destroyed and she immediately listed to starboard—water was leaking in everywhere and her stern began to settle lower in the water. There were gas leaks below deck and the ventilation systems began to shut down. Men who weren't detailed to damage control teams stayed at their stations or near their bunks waiting for orders. A rumor spread through much of the ship that three men were working in the flooding steering room trying to manually stabilize the ship. The fate of the crippled ship and that of her crew were in the hands of these men. The carrier began to turn to port in circles, easy prey for a fatal second strike. Captain Stump told the men in the steering room to stay or abandon their posts—it was *their* decision. They stayed.

I distinctly remember my father telling me as we drove to the local lumber yard in his old Chevy pickup truck how Captain Stump, over the intercom, told the crew "Men, I got you in here and I'll get you out." Forty years later I found the captain's exact words in a book about the *Lexington* and they gave me goose bumps: "This is the Captain speaking. We have taken a torpedo in our stern and the rudder seems badly damaged. Each man must do his job calmly and efficiently. Don't worry! That's my job. I got you in here and I'll get you out."

The *Lexington* began to settle as her steering room flooded. Five submersible pumps were put to use and although her stern was ten feet deeper in the water than normal, she stabilized. Escorted by the heavy cruiser *Minneapolis* and being steered manually the *Lexington* began making her way for the safe waters of Pearl Harbor. But not all was well. Two men are dead, seven are missing and thirty-five have been wounded to varying degrees. My father told me how quiet the ship became the next morning when two of his shipmates were buried at sea. "I remember it like it was yesterday," he told me.

After arriving at Pearl Harbor the *Lex* went into dry dock and seven more bodies were found in the damaged area. Temporary repairs were made and within forty-eight hours the *Lexington* was moving again—this time underway for the Bremerton Navy Yard in Seattle. All of her planes flew away, heading back to the war, leaving my father, Jack and the other machinist mates with little to do. Because the *Lexington's* predecessor of the same name had been sunk Tokyo Rose referred to my father's carrier as "the ghost." Due to the ship's blue camouflage that moniker evolved into the "Blue Ghost." The Japanese were certain that my father's ship had settled beneath the waves and Tokyo Rose announced that the *Blue Ghost* was no more. My father and the rest of the crew who were listening particularly enjoyed that episode of The Zero Hour. But the nickname, the *Blue Ghost*, stuck. On December 23 the *Lexington* arrived back in the states.

The *Lexington* went under extensive repairs at Bremerton for seven weeks and Ken was granted liberty. He followed his heart back to Rhode Island a few days after Christmas wearing the coat to find Shirley Phillips. The lights of downtown Providence provided a perfect setting for the young couple who dined and danced as if there was no war. They went sledding and skating at Roger Williams Park. Nightly, Ken was a guest at the Phillips' modest dinner table and a friendship with Shirley's parents evolved—it felt natural—it was the making of a new family.

My dad told me decades later that while riding the trolley with my mother on a late January afternoon he heard a businessman say to an associate, "I hope this war goes on forever. Business has never been this good."

My father was obviously still angry, or perhaps incredulous at the remark, even after so many years had passed. "Les, I was in full uniform," he told me. "If I wasn't with your mother and grandparents, I would have said something to the man." Being in full uniform in January means that he was wearing the pea coat. But the man's insensitive comment probably stung my father deeper for another reason. The *Lexington* was ready to return to the South Pacific and a week later Ken and Shirley once again said their goodbyes. My mom's parents didn't want this nice young man to return to the war. My father asked Shirley to marry him during this liberty.

The *Lexington* sailed from Bremerton Navy Yard on February 12, 1944, and Rear Admiral Marc Mitscher made her his flagship. My father and the rest on the machinist mates were busy as the American navy pressed the dwindling Japanese Imperial Navy.

In late April the *Lexington's* planes were in action over and near Truk Island in the South Pacific. Along with fuel and ammunition dumps, several buildings were destroyed. A seaplane ramp and a radio station were also heavily damaged.

My mother told me that she swore to my father that she would never be a war widow and as much as she wanted to marry him, they would have to wait until war's end and he had safely returned home. But by the late 1944 the war's situation had changed—Germany was nearly defeated. My father wrote letter after letter trying to persuade my mother to relent. "The war in Europe is almost over, the Japanese navy barely exists and you already know that my ship is unsinkable!" were just some of his pleadings.

On November 5 my father felt the "divine wind" (kamikaze) when a Japanese pilot flew his plane directly at the center of the *Lexington*'s island (the command tower on the right side of an aircraft carrier). The kamikaze's impact struck near the bridge, causing major damage, disabling several 20mm and 40mm batteries. The ship was on fire, but the flames were extinguished within twenty minutes. Forty-two men were killed instantly and another one hundred and thirty-two were wounded. But the flight deck miraculously suffered no damage and operations resumed.

**Kamikaze damage
(parts of Zero engine visible)**

Kamikaze damage

In early February of 1945 the *Lexington's* bombers hit airfields near Tokyo and supported American landings on Iwo Jima. She returned to the Bremerton Navy yard on March 27 for a scheduled overhaul and with no planes to work on Ken and Jack were granted liberty on April 5.

On April 7, 1945, my parents were married in a small ceremony in Providence, Rhode

Island. Jack was the best man. Jack had also fallen in love with a Providence girl that he would soon marry. The *Blue Ghost's* presence was obvious.

After a brief honeymoon, which was a mere few days visiting my father's family on the farm in Pennsylvania, the couple once again parted. My father returned to the *Lexington* on May 12 hoping that the war's end was near and embarked for Pearl Harbor two weeks later. The thought of an invasion of the Japanese mainland was an ugly one; American casualty projections were in the hundreds of thousands.

In early June American pilots destroyed much of the Japanese air power near Saipan. On June 16 the *Lexington* was once again the object of a determined assault from Japanese torpedo planes. Ken, Jack and the other machinist mates worked hours without sleep, keeping *their* pilots in the air. If everyone did their job the war might be over and everyone would go home—wrenches and oil drums were as important as torpedoes and bombs.

Later that month the *Lexington* showed her stuff in the Philippine Sea where her pilots helped to shoot down three hundred Japanese planes clearing the sky of enemy opposition. An enemy carrier and destroyer were sunk. The Battle of Leyte Gulf followed and the attacks on the *Lexington* were desperate and defiantly fierce. What was left of the Imperial Navy was hopelessly attacking like a cornered wounded animal.

In August two American bombs named "Fat Man" and "Little Boy" ended the lives of thousands, spared the lives of many more, and changed the world forever. The war ended three weeks later. My father said goodbye to the *Lexington* in late September. He never saw her again. He was offered some remedial dental work compliments of the navy but he declined. Ken wanted to get home as quickly as possible—my mother was pregnant. He was honorably discharged on October 10 at Lido Beach, Long Island, New York.

My parents rented an apartment in Providence, Rhode Island, and Ken took a job in one of the city's many mills. He was not suited to spend his days closed up in a big building doing the same job day after day. His move from a dairy farm in eastern Pennsylvania to the vastness of the South Pacific had reshaped the way he viewed the world. Whether he understood this or not he was forever changed. On my parents' first wedding anniversary my sister Lenore was born. I would arrive eight years and three weeks later.

My grandparents helped my mother and father buy a house in the suburbs and loaned them five hundred dollars to buy a truck. In return my father took a shovel to the ground each night after work and dug a foundation and full basement, which would support a bedroom and private bathroom for my grandparents. No machines were used. It was all dug by hand. As a little boy I remember how a neighbor or two would come by with a shovel and help dig for an hour or so.

My mother's father, John Phillips, was a stout, aging Irishman who was known for lifting up automobiles instead of using a jack when a friend or a fellow traveler suffered a "blow out" or a flat tire. He was "a tough old Mick." He was a carpenter—a good one. My father told me how "Pops" once threw a Providence building inspector against a newly cured foundation wall after being asked for a bribe. He also told me about how once when they were leaving a Red Sox game at Fenway Park he told his father-in-law, "I'm going to get cigarettes. I'll meet you at the car." When Ken got to the car Pops was in an altercation with another Red Sox fan about the ownership of the vehicle. Pops had been sitting in the man's car and was told to get out. My grandfather refused and a fight ensued. Things cooled down when both parties agreed that it was an innocent mistake. After all, back then every car was black.

As a result of my grandfather's tutelage my father became a self-employed carpenter. In 1960 his truck doors were emblazoned with *"You Can Depend On Ken."* He could now support a family on his own terms. I remember little of Pops except him being an old blind man sitting in our back yard when I was about five. In 1961 there was commotion followed be silence in our home as a man covered by a sheet was carried out of our front door. My sister Lenore sat next to me. I was confused and began nervously laughing. My sister, Lenore, squeezed my hand. I learned about death that night. Pops was gone.

My grandmother, Idell, was Jack's counterbalance. Tiny and dignified she would regale me with stories of having to carry "hot lunches" to her father and other laborers at the turn of the century. I remember she would be sickened at the very mention of milk because she was forced-fed milk as a remedy for a childhood illness. My father adored "Nana." In my teens Nana would pay me ten cents a week to wind her old wall clock and pour for her a nightly glass of "doctor ordered" port wine. My room being across the hall from hers, I would fall asleep listening to her giggles as she watched talk show host Johnny Carson tell "dirty stories" on the Tonight Show and hear her softly playing her harmonica. She showed me how to do centuries-old hand tricks like "One man pickin' Two men choppin." My teenage friends always took time to visit her when they came to the house. As she approached eighty years of age, and after sleeping in a room across the hallway from my bedroom through the sixties and early seventies she became a Beatles' fan. *When I'm Sixty-Four* was her favorite. She left us in 1975 and I secretly placed her harmonica in her casket to take with her on her new journey.

In December of 1945 the *Lexington* sailed home in peaceful waters. One hundred and thirty-eight of her crew did not return with her. Her crew received the Presidential Unit Citation for heroism. My father and the other men were also awarded eleven battle stars representing the major engagements in which they had been engaged. The ship's resume was splendid, having destroyed nearly 850 enemy aircraft and sinking or destroying 300,000 tons of enemy cargo and damaging more than a half million tons of supplies. Her own gunners downed 15 planes. *Lady Lex* had set more records than any other carrier of her class in the history of naval aviation. Two years later she was decommissioned and "mothballed" for over half a decade.

In 1953 she was recommissioned featuring a new "angled" deck which allowed her to launch and receive aircraft simultaneously. The *Blue Ghost* resumed serving our nation in the Pacific and Atlantic Oceans and the Gulf of Mexico until 1991 when she was decommissioned for the last time. The scrap yard beckoned.

My father Ken and I at a Civil War reenactment (1996)

On one of our last Christmases together, I gave my father a scale model of the modernized *Lexington* featuring her new angled deck. He said to me, "Thanks, Les, but that's not her." He was wrong. But I had no right to disturb his memories. The *Blue Ghost* would remain as he remembered her. The coat had been stored in several closets over the decades and I knew I would never wear it again. It didn't matter. It was one of those things you didn't have to explain to anyone. This was a coat that I shared with a special friend.

My father passed away in 1999 just a few months before my first book was published. I wish he had lived to see it. My mother Shirley joined him a decade later. They left very little behind, but it didn't matter to me. I still had the coat after all these years.

On June 15, 1992, the U.S.S. *Lexington* CV-16 was donated by the navy as a floating museum and now operates as the U.S.S. *Lexington* Museum on the Bay in Corpus Christi, Texas. She is the oldest aircraft carrier in the world. The hangar bay where my father worked and sweated for two years will soon be part of the museum. It was time for a piece of her to be returned to its rightful home.

The 70 year-old coat that my father and I shared will be soon on display in a glass case with a nameplate reading "The Pea Coat of Aviation Machinist Mate 2nd class Kenneth Eugene Rolston" on the *Blue Ghost* only a few feet from where he once kept Hellcats and Dauntless Dive Bombers in the air and where he mingled among pilots, machine gunners and his friend, Jack. Aviation Machinist Mate Rolston fulfilled the assignment to which he had been designated and he did it well, as his honorable discharge attests.

Our Pea Coat will be the only identified coat of its kind in the museum's collection. Except for one missing button it is in pristine condition. I hope to see it again one day.

I love you Dad.

The Pea Coat

The U.S.S. *Lexington* today

CV-16 U.S.S. *Lexington,* the *"Blue Ghost"* today.

Sources

National Archives Records Administration

Conversations With My Father, Les Rolston, unpublished

The Story of the U.S.S. *Lexington* **CV-16, WWII Tarawa To Tokyo 1943-46**: Published by the Officers and Men of the U.S.S. *Lexington* as a Permanent Record of the Story of the U/S.S.

Carrier *Lexington*, Text and Contemporary Photographs by Hugh Power, Introduction by Robert J. Cressman, Foreword by Jerry Chipman, Texas A & M University Press, 1996

Blue Ghost Memoirs: U.S.S. CV-16, 1943-45, Otto C. Romanelli, Lt. Cdr. USNR (Ret.), Turner Publishing Company, Paducah, Kentucky, 2002

The Blue Ghost, A Photographic Log and Personal Narrative Of The Aircraft Carrier U.S.S. *Lexington* **In Combat Operation**, Edward Steichen Captain, USNR (ret.), Harcourt, Brace and Company, New York, New York, 1947

Aircraft Carriers of World War II, Color Pictures from National Archives Collection, Website:
<http://www.historylink101.com/ww2_navy/org/aircarr/U.S.S. Lexington/index.html>

MilitaryAircraft.de · Aviation Photography, Ulrich Grueschow, 2005-2013, Website: <http://www.militaryaircraft.de/>

www.ingramcontent.com/pod-product-compliance
Lightning Source LLC
Chambersburg PA
CBHW062114290426
44110CB00023B/2807